Mama Nightshade's

Compendium

of Acquired Magickal Knowledge

Dedicated to those of us who have been true to ourselves, even if it meant being a black sheep.

Special Thanks to:

My Family & Friends

My Coven

The Silver Moon Society

Magickal People of All Denominations

Hecate

Mama Nightshade's Compendium of Acquired Knowledge of Folk Magick.

In this book, I will be sharing knowledge and spells that I have created and adapted for the past thirty years, which is exactly how long I have been a practicing Witch. Many of these spells were inspired by ancient arcane knowledge that has been written in tomes from the 1500's up until the modern era. There are no rules in my Spell collection. There are spells and recipes from almost every Magickal culture that exists, for I am a bookworm and have an addiction to learning- especially about all things Magickal. So, please do not read this expecting me to categorize any of my acquired knowledge as 'Cultural Appropriation' of Magick. I, like most of us in the Southern United States come from an extremely Culturally Diverse genetic background. I do not feel like I have any need to apologize for tapping into any facet of my heritage to draw upon my magickal roots. With that being said, please forgive me for being so blunt and I do hope that you enjoy the fruits of my years of labor.

This book will also be a symphony of chaos, just as it is in my weathered old black binder that I dubbed my Personal Book of Shadows like 20 years ago. The sections will be categorized by Subject (Money, Love, Protection, etc...) and it will be sprinkled with useful knowledge from several different cultures within each section. There will also be a few Chapters that will strictly be sectioned as their historical or cultural roots. Like, for instance Medieval Spells, Hoodoo Spells, Romany Magick, etc... As I previously stated: A Symphony of Chaos. Please enjoy!

Money Magick

This first chapter will be the one about money or material gain, as it is a concern that is pretty much paramount for most of us with the world in the state of madness that it currently Identifies as. Money, unfortunately, is extremely important to us these days. We have not yet reached the times of a financial burden free utopia that the Star Trek franchise promises. We are still slaves to the almighty greenback and must have money in order to survive in these modern times, as people in the world today are not exactly as practical and able bodies as our forefathers were.

Money Spells can range from very simple to extremely complex. The goal of these spells is to bring about the opportunity to gain money or material wealth. You won't be able to magickally summon a fully stocked bank vault with any of these spells. That's not exactly how it works. These spells will basically grease the cogs on the wheel of destiny, making attaining funds easier, or by clearing a path for you to get what you need. Most of the spells that I have accrued do not require much to be enacted. I am a firm believer in the power of will and manifestation of opportunities. Like all spells, these work better with more intent. That's how manifestation works.

*Money Dolls

Cut out the shape you desire from green flannel. The doll can be a person, an elephant, a Leprechaun, Mermaid or whatever you envision.

Stuff it with dill, moss and a few coins. Cinnamon may also be added if you like. Sew it up and embellish it as you desire.

Anytime you make a doll, remember that it will always work better if you 'Baptize' it in the name of who or what it is supposed to represent. This can be done by anointing it and declaring its name in the presence of the Goddess or Gods or may be done in your magick circle when consecrating your other Altar Tools.

Talk to your doll, tell it your troubles and request advice before you go to sleep. Pay attention to your dreams, the answer is probably there.

*Elaborate Money Doll Spell

Cut out the outline of your doll with green fabric. Sew it up with gold thread, leaving a gap in the stitching to stuff it.

Make the stuffing from comfrey, king fern, kings root, you can also add some Hell Money or Spirit Money and a little green rice. (There will be a recipe for the green rice in this section)

Write a little note on parchment to the effect of:

'I require_____(amount) plus some extra. I need this immediately to meet my needs.'

Stick it inside the doll.

Use Money oil to dress the doll, or fast luck oil if you're in a hurry.

Wrap the doll in a green cloth. Anoint it daily with Oil until your need has been met, then burn the doll.

Repeat from scratch as needed.

*Corn Husk Dolly Money Spell

On the New Moon, make a doll from dried corn husks, tying it with green yarn or string and sticking a dollar bill inside.

Visualize her pregnant with riches.

Wrap the doll in velvet and hide her in a dark and safe place so that money can germinate and grom like seedlings.

When the full moon arrives, burn the doll and pray or repeat incantations. This should bring swift results.

*Dry Money Incense

Grind and powder some cinnamon, nutmeg, cloves and lemon zest. Sprinkle it on a lit charcoal disk and visualize the results you seek. Be careful with this one and do it in a very well-ventilated area and avoid getting the smoke in your eyes. It might make your eyes burn horribly if you're not careful. Rub your hands together in the smoke (Carefully) and visualize the money coming to you.

*Money Oil

Add powdered Bayberry and Oakmoss to Sweet Almond Oil. Add bits of gold leaf flakes or foil (Glitter will work in a pinch) Rub between your hands as needed or use to dress candles or anoint yourself or items.

*Money Plant Spells

Purchase a small potted plant. Gently rub prosperity oil or luck oil on its leaves. Reanoint the leaves with this oil once a month. Remember to offer libations or offerings as needed. Especially when the plant seems to be working on your behalf.

*Basic Money Botanical Candle

Hold a green candle and charge it with your desires. Hollow out its base and pack it full of basic money drawing herbs or powders. Burn it in a money spell.

*Radiant Symbol Candle Spell

Carve your name into a green candle. Carve a symbol to represent money onto it.

Hold the candle and focus your energy into it.

Dress and embellish the candle with money drawing oils and powders and then burn.

*Fast Cash Spell for Money Growth

Carve and dress a green candle to express your desires.

Place it on a saucer and arrange coins around the base.

Light the candle and say:

'Money grow, Money flow

Candle burn, watch me Earn

Bright Flames shine

I want what's mine!'

*Tulip Bulb Spell

Place a tulip bulb in a conjure bag and secure it in a safe place. Tulips are said to protect against poverty.

*Trinka Five Gypsy Chant

Works alone or with candle spells.

(Very effective, I use it often and can vouch)

'Trinka Five, Trinka Five

Ancient Spirits come alive

Bring me money, bring it fast

Trinka Five, make it last!"

*Spell to Land a Job

After submitting a resume or filling out an application, carve the name of the company onto a green candle. Carve your name and the Tiwaz Rune symbol onto a red candle.

Light them and burn them for thirty minutes on a Thursday. Snuff them out.

Light them both every Thursday for fifteen minutes until the job is yours.

After you get hired, leave a small bowl of milk on your doorstep as an offering.

*Simple Cash at Hand Spells- Quick and easy money spells

-Anoint all your dollar bills with magnet oil or return-to-me oil before spending so it returns to you.

-Burn dried onion skins on the stove to bring money to you when in need.

-Burn two garlic peels in the kitchen to keep money in the house.

-Rub two drops of bergamot essential oil into your hands.

-Put aspen leaves into a conjure bag and carry them with you.

-Put a cinnamon stick, grains of paradise (or green rice will work) and five coins in a conjure bag and keep with you.

-Place seven coins in a charm bag with violet leaves and cinquefoil to generate wealth.

-Sprinkle powdered ginger in your pocket, purse or wallet.

-Blend skunk cabbage (or regular cabbage) with bay laurel to stimulate an influx of wealth.

-Blow powdered cinnamon out your front door on the first of the month to increase wealth.

-Carry or wear green tourmaline to attract money.

-Bury an acorn on the dark moon to receive a money infusion soon.

-Eat Goose meat on September 29th, this is Michael, The Arch Angel's Feast Day.

Sprinkle gold magnetic sand over two lodestones and put in a red flannel conjure bag with a dollar bill and a piece of pyrite.

Leave coins or spare change on your doorstep, what you put forth comes back three-fold.

*To Obtain Money

Fill a cauldron halfway with water and drop a silver coin into it. Put it in a place where the moonlight shines onto it. Gently sweep your hands over it, symbolically gathering up the moon's silver. Say:

'Lovely Lady of the Moon

Bring me your wealth and bring it soon.

Fill my hands with silver and gold

All you give, my hands can hold.'

Repeat this twice more then pour the water onto the earth.

*Money Spell

Do this spell at the proper Jupiter day and hour.

Anoint a green candle and a white candle with oil.

Set on the table nine inches apart and say:

'Money, money come to me

In abundance three times three

May I be enriched in the best of ways

Harming none on its way

This I accept, so mote it be

Bring me money, three times three.'

Do this spell on a Thursday and repeat for eight days following. Move the candles an inch closer together each night. When they are finally touching, the spell is done.

*More money manifesting spells

-Sprinkle cinnamon in your wallet.

-Hollow out an acorn and fill it with cinnamon, thyme and gold flakes. Seal it closed with green wax and keep it safe as an amulet.

-Stick a garlic clove with nine pins and hang it near your front door to protect you from poverty.

-Fill a small bowl with equal parts of sugar, salt and rice. Mix thoroughly and stick an open safety pin in the center.

-Rub a green candle with honey, sprinkle with cinnamon and a dab or orange juice or zest. Light and ask Saint Expedite for quick money.

Candle Magick

Candle Magick is probably the most versatile type of Spell Craft, as you can pretty much do any kind of Spell with the right candle. The key to the biggest part of the magick associated with candles comes from color association. Candles provide what is called Sympathetic Magick. This is basically the concept of 'Like attracts Like'. In other words, Sympathetic Magick is where an object of representation is used as a proxy in your spell. Something to represent your spell's target and/or desired outcome and effects.

With Candle Magick, we generally select a candle whose color is relevant to our needs. For instance, a green candle would work best for money or fertility spells, as green is the color for growth. After choosing an appropriate colored candle, the candle will need to be prepared for use. This usually involves carving symbols or words into it to represent what we are seeking. For a money spell, maybe carving a dollar sign would work well for you.

Once we have carved symbols, words or names into it, the candle would then need to be anointed. This is where we use an oil that is appropriate for our spell work to dress the candle. To do this, I usually splash a little oil into my hands and rub it onto the candle. Direction of application is very important when doing this. If you are doing a spell to bring something to you or draw something into your life you will need to start at the top of the candle where the wick is and rub it downward towards the bottom.

To rid yourself of an unwanted situation, person or trait, works in reverse. You will start at the bottom and rub the oil up towards the top, away from you. These actions all play an important role in making the spell work. The way you do everything in the spell, even simple gestures can have a huge impact on the outcome. The most important thing to remember, aside from being safe and responsible, is that INTENT is what it's all about. No matter how few supplies you have, the simplest spell can have the biggest impact if you have a good amount of *intent*. This is how we truly manifest our goals into reality. Our willpower is a very powerful thing when channeled.

Candle Color Associations

Red- strength, energy, sex, passion, courage, protection, defensive magick. Element of Fire. Life and Death (Red is the color of Blood)

Pink- love, friendship, compassion, relaxation, emotional unions, baby girls.

Orange- attraction, energy, creativity, motivation burn to attract specific influences or objects.

Yellow- intellect, confidence, divination, communication, eloquence, travel, movements, stimulates your conscious mind. Element of Air. Gender neutral babies.

Green- money, prosperity, employment, fertility, healing, growth. Element of Earth.

Blue- healing, peace, psychism, patience, happiness, awakens the psychic mind. Element of Water. Baby boys.

Purple- power, healing, spirituality, meditation. Religion enhances spiritual activity, increases magickal power.

White- protection, purification, consecration. Can be used in place of any color. It also represents the moon.

Black- banishing, absorbing negativity, casting out baneful energies. It also represents outer space.

Brown- animal magick, used with red for animal protection, used with blue for animal healing, green for animal fertility, etc...

Types of candles and their uses

*7 Day Candles- good for seven-day spells, love drawing or luck spells.

*3 Day Candles- Three-day spells and house blessings.

*Tapers- good for any type of spell-work. Beeswax candles work particularly well.

*Chime Candles- 4 inches tall and are generally what you'll find if you look up Spell Candles. Works like Tapers but a little faster for when we don't have a lot of time.

*Votive Candles- good for all spells that don't require a long burn-time.

*Tea Light Candles- good for very quick spells.

Notes to remember:

*Hand Dipped Candles are great, a little pricey though, so not exactly a requirement.

*Inscribing them with plenty of symbols can be tricky so try to runes in place of words.

*After anointing or dressing your candles, herbs may be dusted onto them or rubbed into the surface for extra potency.

*Never, ever leave a lit candle unattended. If you are in a hurry, reschedule your ritual or use a smaller candle.

*Be sure to use a fire safe surface or candle holder. I learned this the hard way, early on.

Love Magick

This section will be dedicated to matters of the heart. Love Magick can be a very tricky thing, as most people think that you can just wave a magick wand and make someone fall in love with you, regardless of the repercussions. Fortunately, it isn't quite that simple, and I say fortunately because the world would be horrible if every love spell worked like that, every time. Sure, the heart wants what the heart wants, but the heart can be a fickle thing sometimes, as it turns out.

Real Love Spells don't work like that. When we cast a love spell this is what happens: We open ourselves or someone else up to give or receive love. Love spells are not like emotional roofies. They're more like emotional primers. We are priming ourselves to be the recipients of the love of another.

In this section, I will be listing some of the spells that I have come across over the years, and some of them may seem a little extreme or far-fetched. But for the sake of Pseudoscience, I will be adding them, nonetheless. Also, know that I have not attempted all the spells listed in this book. Many of them were inspired but not required. Some of them will sound pretty disgusting, as well. I found several of them in obscure volumes of medieval magick. But as I stated before- it's for the sake of pseudoscience. This book will contain many secret rites that I have not actually needed and therefore are untested, so if you attempt them, you are doing so at your own risk.

Another thing worth mentioning is that this section will contain all types of love spells. Some encourage love, but also some discourage it. By titling this section Love Magick, I mean to say that we will be looking at all types of spells concerning love.

*Doll Binding Spell

Create a pair of dolls from fabric, one to represent each partner.

Stuff them with dried herbs associated with love, like rose petals and lavender.

Rub them with oils of the same type.

Dress and ornate them, adding beads if possible, making a knot after each one.

Tie the dolls facing together, face to face with red string, yarn or ribbons. This will help to protect and preserve romance and encourage passion.

Wrap them in fabric and keep them in a safe place for as long as you wish this romance to last.

*Apple Binding Spell

Cut an apple horizontally to reveal the star in the center that is made up of the seeds.

Spread each half with honey.

Take a lock of hair from each person's head and braid them together.

Place the braided hair in between the two halves, sandwiching it with the honey.

Bind the halves together with red ribbon, making several knots.

Bury this Love Apple in the earth in a romantic spot, like where you had a date or somewhere beautiful.

*The Spell of Nine

Carve your name and the name of your beloved onto a candle.

Blend honey, rose water, rose petals, a dash of cinnamon and red pepper seeds together and put on a saucer.

Dress the candle with an appropriate oil and then roll it in the mixture on all sides.

Light the candle at exactly 9pm for exactly 9 minutes for 9 consecutive nights.

At the end of the last 9 minutes on the last of 9 nights, take whatever is left of this and tie it up in a piece of fabric with 9 ribbons.

Bury this packet at a crossroads, in a cemetery, or under your front porch.

*Love Conjuring Charms

*Druid Conjure Bag for Men- place Holly leaves and berries in a conjure bag and carry on your person.

*Druid Love Conjure- fill a conjure bag with elecampane, mistletoe and vervain.

*Artemis Charm Bag- fill a bag with a silver moon charm, wormwood, and mugwort.

*Love Drawing Sachet- fill a sachet with rose petals and catnip. Wear it over your heart like a necklace.

*Love Drawing Sachet v.2- fill a sachet with vervain, rosemary, lavender and rose petals.

*Love Letter Spell- write an invisible love letter on a bay leaf and keep it in an envelope.

*Love Powder- dust powdered orrisroot on your Beloved's clothes or body to arouse interest.

*Love Potion- steep fresh basil leaves in wine with rose petals. Strain and drink to open yourself up for love.

*Nutmeg Love Potion- carry a whole nutmeg in your armpit for 48 hours. Grind it up and add it to a bottle of red wine. Serve it to your Beloved.

*Sandalwood Seduction- men are advised to wear sandalwood scent to elicit sexual desire from a potential mate.

*Place a pinch of orrisroot in each corner of your home to encourage love.

*Carry a whole orrisroot for success in love.

*Procure a lock of hair from the one you love and wear it in your hat to attract them.

*Paint a wishbone gold and add it to a conjure bag with 6 grains of paradise and red rose petals.

*Carry an Amethyst as an Amulet to attract women.

*Oregano Spell for Heartache

The scent of Oregano is said to help you forget about old lovers. Burn the dried herb as incense or use the essential oil.

*Honeysuckle Heartache Remover

Bathe in honeysuckles, you can use fresh flowers or essential oil. Light a white candle anointed with the oil and let it burn while you bathe. This discourages unhealthy nostalgia.

*Chocolate Love Potion

Chocolate is renowned as a powerful aphrodisiac. Serve some hot chocolate to your lover. It has a chemical in it called phenylethylamine, the very same chemical that our brains release during sex.

*Hydromel

Beverages made from fermented honey may be the most ancient intoxicant. Mead is a hydromel, as is Ethiopian Honey Wine. These beverages enhance the potency of spells that encourage seduction.

*Damballa Marital Assistance Spell

Damballa, a Dahomey serpent deity is among the most primordial and powerful voodoo spirits. Along with his wife, Ayida Wedo, he sustains and maintains the Earth. He is the proverbial benevolent and wise serpent spirit and ancient. He does not speak but hisses only. If a married couple honors him together he will help them maintain their happiness. This can be done by creating an altar for him in your bedroom. Feed Damballa every Thursday white foods like milk and eggs. Set white and silver candles on the altar for him.

*Lover's Knot Spell

During the wedding reception, pull a thread from the bride's dress and from the groom's outfit.

Tie the two threads together, knotting love, devotion and happiness.

Preserve this knot in a safe place, a Lover's Knot cannot be undone.

A cool idea is to make bracelets from them to wear, one for each of you. Every time you look at them, you will feel the love and happiness that you felt on the day that you got married.

*Japanese Bridal Preparation Spell

In traditional Japanese rituals, the bride is marinated in flowers and warm scented oils including jasmine, frangipani and roses.

Depending on how wealthy the bride's family is, these combined cleansing and purifying spells can last several days.

*Bridal Protection Spells

Sew herbs into the hem of a bride's wedding dress or belt to bring love and romance to the marriage. Ideal herbs for this are: clover, elecampane, lavender, and powdered mistletoe.

*Bridal Protection Conjure Bag- fill a red silk bag with cowrie shells, small horseshoes, a clove of garlic, red ribbon and silver charms.

*Protection Garter Spell- The bridal garter was originally a protective garment, intended to protect the bride from spiritual attack, as well as being a functional part of her wardrobe. For maximum protection, instead of wearing a blue one, wear a red one with a silver charm sewn onto it.

*Bridal Shoe Protection- wrap a needle and a pinch of salt in a piece of red silk. Place it into the bride's right shoe to promote her magickal wellbeing.

*Happy Marriage Spells

*Duck Spell- Ducks mate for life, and a pair of mandarin ducks serves as a lucky marriage charm, in hopes that the happy couple will be able to mirror their devotion to each other. They represent faithfulness and fidelity. Place an image of a Pair of Mandarin Ducks or a matching pair of figurines in a prominent place in your home to radiate happiness and devotion.

*Handfasting Broom- The broom plant is a plant of fertility and growth. Create a ritual broom for a handfasting ceremony to mark the sacred space encompassing the couple.

*Rosemary- The couple should dip a rosemary stick into their first drink as a married couple and sip it from the same cup together. This will preserve the love and happiness.

*Happy Marriage Tree Magick- Surround your home with Magnolia Trees or Pine Trees (or both) to shield and preserve your happy marriage.

*Groom's Potion

Cook eggs with honey, cinnamon, cloves, mace and nutmeg. Mix two parts of this with one part of a good wine. Serve it to the Groom, it is said to increase vigor on the wedding night.

*Couple's Potion

Steep Myrtle in white wine. The bride and groom should drink this together from one glass to ensure fidelity, romance fertility. Also used to beseech Aphrodite's blessings upon their union.

*Honeymoon Potion

Inspiring the Origins of the term Honeymoon, Teutonic Brides were fed honey beer daily for a full month following the handfasting ceremony. This kept the bride relaxed, happy and more responsive sexually.

Fidelity Spells-

*Fidelity Candle- powder caraway seeds, licorice root and cumin. Add this blend to grapeseed oil. Carve a figure candle to represent your partner. Dress it with this oil and burn it.

*Elderberry Fidelity Spell- Carrying Elderberry trigs and berries guard against the temptations of infidelity.

*Locket Spell- Wear a locket containing a picture of your Beloved with a lock of their hair over your heart to encourage faithfulness.

*Lodestones- Place two matching lodestones in a sachet with plenty of skullcap. Wrap up in fabric and place it deep inside your Lover's pillow.

*Sock Spell- Tie a knot in your Lover's unwashed sock and hide it under your side of the bed or near it under the rug.

Explicit Spells for Love and Lust

As a side note, most of these should probably not be attempted. I added them because I found them interesting and novel, but I would not attempt most of these. Alterations could be made to make them more sanitary and safer, but that's your call, and do any of it at your own risk.

*Sex Ball Spell

Warm up red wax in your hands until it is pliable.

Roll it into a ball.

Add a few of your lover's pubic hairs and a few drops of your menstrual blood into it, or blood from your finger.

Knot your intentions into a cord and add this to it as well.

Roll the ball in your hands until it is smooth and evenly rounded.

Hold it in your right hand and charge it.
Hide it in a safe place or carry it with you.
This Spell is to keep the Sex Good!

*To Cause Impotence

This spell requires semen, but not yours. Only your mate's.

Attain this, however you see fit (Usually the traditional way).

Add goofer dust to it. Wrap this paste into a piece of fabric or paper.

Bury it in the earth where your partner is sure to step over it. Nothing will happen if he/she/they are faithful. But if they try to have sex with someone else, this will cause impotence and insanity (temporarily).

*Love Leash

Measure a cord the length of your husband's erect penis. Keep safe until you can soak it in his sexual fluids (semen). Make knots in it and put it in a secret place.

*Binding Love Leash

After having sex, retain the cloth that you both have used to clean up with. Tie it in seven knots. Place a rock inside of it and knot all around it. Toss or drop it into a river. Make an appeal or petition to the river Spirit to protect your love. Only the person who created this charm can break this spell by fishing it out of the river and undoing it.

*Hoodoo Ligature

Trim a string to match the length of your husband's erect penis.

After you have sex, secretly soak some of his semen into it.

Let him fall asleep and tie a loose loop into the center of the rope. Call out his name and when he responds (while sleeping) tighten the knot. Once should do the trick but you can do this up to seven times, creating a witch's ladder type charm.

Keep it in a safe and secret place. If you think he might see it, keep it in a Nation Bag.

*A nation bag is like a conjure bag that must not be opened and looked into once filled and tied, or else the spell will be reversed. It must be consecrated and have personal effects inside of it.

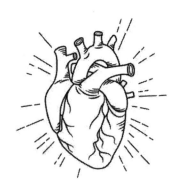

Spells for a More Blissful Union

*Heartache and Stress Spell- The Other Woman

Go to a crossroad barefoot with your hair down.

Once you're there, pick up a pebble and place it under your left armpit.

Say: *'As this pebble can be removed from this crossroad, so may that other woman be removed from my Lover's heart.'*

Go to a second crossroads and pick up another pebble. Place it underneath your right arm and repeat your wish.

With both pebbles, go to a third crossroads and pick up another pebble. Stick this one between your breasts and repeat your wish again.

Return home, but before you enter your house, drop all the pebbles into a gutter.

*Spell to Remedy Marital Problems-

Fill a glass with sea salt, rose water and holy water. Drop your wedding ring in it and let it soak overnight. Recite your wedding vows as you remember them.

In-law Spells

*In-Law Oregano Spell-

Oregano keeps meddlesome in-laws at bay. Smudge your home with it before they come visit. It also helps to smudge their picture with it regularly to guard against dysfunctional issues.

*In-Law Spell #2

If they won't change their ways or stay away, you can make them a little nicer towards you by grinding up some of your fingernail clippings and brewing them with your coffee grounds, then serving it to them.

*In-Law Spell #3

If none of these other methods work, you can try to burn some Queen of the Meadow, also known as Bridewort, to help relieve tensions between them and yourself.

Love Amulets

*Carry:

*A key tied to a red ribbon as an amulet to attract love.

*A small bird fetish or figure in a red silk bag.

*Aniseed

*2 potatoes, carved with your initials and your Beloved's. They are then tied with a red string or ribbon. If planted, your love will grow as the plant does.

Healing Spells

*Candle Distance Spell

Carve a white candle to reflect the person in need of healing.

Soak hyssop in olive oil and then use the oil to dress the candle.

Burn the candle, this is usually accompanied by reciting psalms or other sacred verses.

*Peppermint Distance Healing Spell

Place Peppermint leaves on top of a picture of the patient.

Charge a blue candle with your desired outcome.

Carve and dress the candle as desired.

Burn it beside the picture of them. When the candle burns down, dispose of the peppermint leaves.

Repeat as needed with fresh leaves each time.

*Talisman Distance Healing Spell

To promote long distance healing, charge crystals with healing energy (Reiki). Then give them to the spell's target as a talisman. Choose any crystal that feels right to you; however, these work the best: Alexandrite, Herkimer Diamonds, Lodestones, Moonstone, Pearls and Quartz Crystals.

*Rosemary Infusion of Power

Washing your hands with an infusion of rosemary magickally enhances all healing spells you perform. Create an infusion by pouring boiling water over fresh rosemary. Allow it to cool and then strain it. This should be done immediately before doing your healing spell or can be bottled and refrigerated for later use. Freshly picked rosemary from your garden works the very best, and it is extremely easy to grow.

*<u>Mistletoe Ring-</u> carve a ring from mistletoe and wear it to ward off illness.

*<u>Amber Asthma Spell-</u>

Wear Amber around your throat to heal asthma and prevent attacks (in the form of a necklace- obviously) Amber, beaded tightly in the form of a necklace is believed to absorb body heat and therefore treat fevers and chills.

*<u>Mugwort Anti-Infection Spell-</u>

Hang mugwort over the entrance doors of your home to ward off infectious disease. It can be tied with twine and hung over the top of the door upside down, like a tiny little bouquet.

*Thyme Anti-Infection Spell-

Burn Thyme so that its aroma permeates an area so that it wards off infectious disease. You can also add some to your sage smudge bundles, this is like hitting two birds with one stone, by preventing illness and negativity.

*Moonwater Healing Potion- place sacred objects into an iron cauldron or a glass bowl. (Sacred objects include- crucifix, pentacle, amulet or talisman) Cover them with pure spring water. Expose this to moonlight overnight. Works best if done on a full moon or during an eclipse.

*Pomanders

Choose a beautiful orange or grapefruit that is healthy.

Carefully pierce it with holes, making sure to only pierce the skin, not the inner flesh.

You can incorporate designs when doing this, like a connect the dots image.

Stick a clove into each hole.

To put the spell into effect, focus on your desired goal while piercing the holes and adding the cloves. Murmur sacred verses, prayers, chants or affirmations while doing this.

Roll the Pomander in orrisroot and/or cinnamon.

Tie it up with red ribbons and hang it in your home to repel and remove illnesses.

*Oshun's Women's Healing Spell

Depending on which legend you hear, Oshun is Yemaya's (The Sea Goddess or Loa) daughter or sister. She has dominion over the abdominal area and the female reproductive organs. Petition her for healing and offer her a glass of pure spring water and fresh honey, tasting the honey before offering it to her. Light five golden candles and request her assistance.

*Triple Leaf Triple Goddess Spell- a

A three-leaf clover is said to represent the stages of a woman's life; Maidenhood, Motherhood and Cronehood. Carry a real one or a replica as a talisman to promote optimum health at all stages of your life.

*Yemaya's Female Recovery Spell

The Orisha, Yemaya has dominion over all woman's issues, therefore she may be petitioned renewal and rejuvenation. Offer her a glass of water with sea salt and a slice of poundcake with dark molasses poured over it. Dedicate a blue 7-day candle to Yemaya and tell her what you need, then ask her for her assistance.

*Magick Grass Headache Spell

Pluck a few blades of fresh green grass.

Chant the following charm while making the sign of the horns behind your back:

'It isn't the grass I take, but the power I make. Go away and stay away from me, headache! So, Mote it be!'

Wrap the glass in a solid white cloth and hold it against your brow with your eyes closed for a few minutes.

**WARNING- Please Don't Do This One. (Seriously- Ew.)*

*Papua New Guinea Coconut/Semen Spell

Grate some coconut into a dish. Mix it with a little semen and feed it to those wishing to receive magickal safety from an epidemic.

*Oye's Headache Remedy

The Orisha Oye cure headaches. This spell is great for migraines.

Oye wears a crown with 9 charms: Pick, Hoe, Gourd, Lightning Bolt, Scythe, Shovel, Rake, Axe and Mattock (Pickaxe). Collect them for her as a petition for ending your headaches. Burn a small purple candle each time you collect a charm. When you have all Oye's charms burn a purple 7-day candle in her honor. Offer her a glass of red wine and the charms then make your request.

*Eyebright Anti-Depression Spell-

Create an infusion with eyebright and boiling water. Let it cool and use it as eyewash.

*Thyme Pillow- stuff dream pillows with lavender and thyme to ward off melancholy.

*Hypochondria Potion-

This magick potion relieves the stress

And anxiety of hypochondria. Steep lemon balm in wine for several hours then strain. One glass helps stabilize the condition.

*Chesnut Pain Relief Spell- carry a buckeye or a chestnut in your pocket to help relieve arthritis pain.

*Copper Garter- attach copper charms to a red garter (or belt) and wear it for arthritis pain.

*Potato Spell- keep a small potato in your pocket for arthritis pain.

*Raw Beef Anti-Pain Spell for Isolated Pain- Place a fresh, raw beefsteak on the afflicted area of your body until that area starts to sweat. The sweat must be in contact with the beef, for this is how the pain is transferred out of your body and into the beef. Give the meat to a dog to eat, but do not eat it yourself. It will cancel out the spell if you do.

*Stone Pain Removal Spell- hold a stone or a smooth rock in your hand and visualize it absorbing your pain. Wrap barley straw around the stone while maintaining visualization. Throw the stone into living water that is flowing away from you.

Banishing Spells

Banishing spells remove someone or something from your presence, often permanently. Obviously, these spells can be used to help to drive toxic or unwanted people away from you, and entities or energies can also be banished. Other things can be banished, too. Habits, situations, mind-sets like low self-esteem and anger issues, and blockages or things that are holding you back can also be banished from your life. Hell, depending on how you word it, you could even banish financial difficulties. This section will feature several Banishing Spells and recipes to aid in them. These will not really be in any kind of order. Symphony of Chaos, that's kind of my thing.

*Banish Evil Spell

You will need three things for this spell; a hammer, a rock and a coffin nail (or a 2–3-inch construction nail)

Hammer the nail against the rock. Do not try to pierce the rock, as it will probably shatter or make you smash your thumb. Just hit it hard enough to make a score in the face of the rock 3 times. Visualize what you are banishing while hammering.

Bury the rock far away from where you frequent or reside.

Carry the nail in a red conjure bag, together with some crossroads dirt or graveyard dust.

*Banishing Powder

Banishing powder can be sprinkled on clothes, into the shoes of someone you'd like to see gone or sprinkled into the path of an unwanted visitor. Banishing powder will increase the power of any other banishing magick and can be sprinkled on the candles around your altar when doing other banishing spells.

Grind up black pepper, cayenne, cinnamon, sea salt and sulfur. Mix. Other ingredients can include ground up bay leaves, rep pepper seeds and sage powder.

*Banishing Oil

The same ingredients as listed above, ground to a fine powder. Cover with Castor oil and let sit in a dark place for at least 3 days. Strain and dilute with olive oil.

*Hot Foot Powder

This Hoodoo recipe is pretty similar to banishing powder but works especially well on annoying people. I sometimes add a little graveyard dust for extra potency.

Mix black pepper, cayenne pepper, black salt or sea salt and sulfur.

*A Japanese twist is added to another version, called *Sayonara Powder*. Just ass Wasabi powder and ground ginger to it.

*Coffee Grounds Banishing Spell

Gather the dirt from your target's footprint or from under a chair they've sat in or a bed they've slept in.

Combine the dirt with ground sassafras, cayenne pepper and used coffee grounds. This can be sprinkled on the doorstep to keep them away.

*Foot Track Banishing Spell

Follow the target of your spell, discreetly observing their footprints.

When you see a clear and distinct left footprint, dig it up in its entirety.

Take it home in a bag, then transfer it to a glass jar or bottle, being very careful not to spill any.

Seal the jar or bottle tightly and add a wax seal to it if you like.

Take this to a stream or a river running away from you, in the opposite direction of where you live.

Turning your back to the water, throw it over your left shoulder without looking, being very careful not to hit anything or anyone that you shouldn't.

Walk away without looking back once.

*Traditional Four Thieves Vinegar Recipe

The legend of the four thieves says that during the black plague of medieval times, four brothers from a poor family would go out and rob homes and the grave of the deceased. Despite being exposed to the plague many times over, these men never got sick. When they were finally caught and questioned by authorities about why they never contracted the illness, they claimed that the remedy came from a vinegar and herb concoction that their herbalist parents made. It was said to have been passed down for many generations.

Four thieves' vinegar has many uses and is still in use by many. In medieval times, it was used as a potion to allegedly cure the plague, but currently it is incorporated into a lot of hoodoo spells that I know of for a fact. I'm not saying that an ancient salad dressing recipe is gonna save your life, but I personally know that it adds an extra punch to many different types of spells, especially protective ones.

The original ingredients were cider vinegar, sage, clove, rosemary and wormwood.

Other versions have rue, mint, garlic, thyme and lavender.

One version of it that I make includes graveyard dust, so just don't eat it on your side salad. Here are some spells that use it:

*Rub Four Thieves Vinegar on their doorknob while visualizing them leaving.

*Four Thieves Banishing Spell for unwanted solicitors or collectors

Place a business card inside of a shot glass. If you don't have one, draw one up using the contact info you have.

Fill the glass with Four Thieves Vinegar.

Leave glass standing in a discreet place for as long as necessary.

*FTV Banishing Spell-

Write your target's name on a piece of paper. Soak it in Four Thieves Vinegar (FTV). Fold the paper and bury it in a flowerpot, ideally filled with graveyard dirt. Plant a cactus on top if it and keep it by your front door.

*Marie Laveau's Four Thieves Vinegar Banishment

Write your target's name on a square piece of paper nine times.

Cover and cross each one with your own, saying:

'I cross you; I cover you; I command you; I compel you to _____.'

Place in a bottle or jar and fill with the vinegar, then seal it tightly.

You must then dispose of it, usually this is done by throwing it into running water over your left shoulder, but you can adapt this part to your own needs.

*Four thieves banishing spell for harassment

Sprinkle FTV over sea salt or kosher salt.

Blend well and allow it to dry out completely. Put it in a conjure bag until ready to use.

When the target of this spell next visits or is encountered, sprinkle the salt discreetly in their wake as they depart from you.

*Four Thieves Nine Night Banishing Spell

Each night, for nine consecutive nights, write your target's name on a piece of brown craft paper, with a brief command like 'go home!' or whatever works for you.

Sprinkle the paper with a banishing powder.

Add one of the target's nail clippings, a hair, or a thread from their clothing.

Burn everything, place the ashes in a bottle of Four Thieves Vinegar.

On the ninth night, wrap the bottle tightly in black cloth, securing it with a cord.

Make nine knots, stating again each time, your desire for them to be gone from your life.

Throw this bottle into running water or a cemetery and return home a different route than which you came from.

*Garlic Banishment Spell

Hang a braid of 12 garlic heads over the front door to banish jealous people and the Evil Eye.

*Hit The Road Spell

Fill your pockets with salt in anticipation of the person's departure.

Accompany the person as he or she departs, walking a step behind them to the edge of your property, discreetly sprinkling salt in their wake.

When the person has gone and can no longer see you, take the broom and sweep the salt away, always sweeping away from the direction of your home.

Quietly murmur their name, alternatively praying and petitioning that they do not return, and commanding and compelling them to never come back.

Variations of this spell can include black salt and cayenne pepper for added potency.

*Nettle Banishing Spell-

Burn nettles while focusing on your desires to accomplish the banishment.

*The 'I Banish You with a Gift' Spell

Sprinkle any banishing powder formula onto the dirt of a very nice potted plant.

Sprinkle some powder under the top layer of dirt too, so it isn't that noticeable.

Give this potted plant to your target as a gift. The idea is to get them to take it into their home, activating the spell and compelling them not to want to be in your presence.

*Onion Banishing Spell

Choose an onion whose appearance somehow reminds you of the intended target. Traditionally round ones represent women, whereas pointy ones represent men.

When you have found your onion, carefully hollow out a hole in it, being careful to retain the piece you removed so that you can plug it back up.

Write your target's name five times on a small slip of paper.

Stuff this inside the little onion hole, and then plug it back up with your little onion stopper.

The next time the target leaves your house, discreetly roll the onion in the wake of their exit path before anyone else has a chance to walk over the threshold.

Focus your mind on their imminent departure.

Do not bring the onion back into your home but dispose of it far away.

*Get Out of my House Spell

Construct a small doll using personal items belonging to the target.

Write their name on a small slip of paper.

Pin this to the doll like a name tag.

Soak the doll's feet in banishing oil.

Wrap the doll in black cloth, folding away from you.

Keep it in a safe place, anointing the feet daily with the banishing oil, secretly telling it what you'd like the target to hear.

As soon as the banishment has taken effect, dispose of the doll away from your home. Do not bring it back into your house.

*Simple Cotton Ball Banishment-

Soak a cotton ball in Banishing Oil and slip it into the target's pocket or handbag.

*19-Day Spare Clothing Banishment

To encourage someone to depart, obtain an article of their clothing, even if it's just a sock or a scarf.

Cut a thin strip of fabric from the clothing article and stuff it into a glass bottle.

Write the person's name, along with a distant location on a slip of paper and draw a circle around the name.

Stick this paper into the glass bottle with the cloth and ass salt, sulfur, chili pepper and any banishing powder formula.

Seal it up tightly and allow it to sit in a quiet dark place for nine days.

On the tenth day, take the bottle to a stream with the water flowing away from you and throw it in. You will have results within nine more days.

*Banish Gossip Spell

Place bay leaves, calendula blossoms and a small metal padlock into a conjure bag and carry to stop people from gossiping about you.

*Gag Root Spell

Lobelia, also called gag root or puke weed carried on your person is said to stop people who speak ill of you behind your back.

*The *Mother* of all Banishing Spells

You will need some protection herbs of your own choosing, an image of the target, or something infused with their energy (hair, handwriting, nail clippings, clothing, etc...) and a fireproof container or cauldron.

Place your herbs into the cauldron and start the fire. Feed it so that it doesn't die out very fast. Place the image or personal items into the fire and say:

'By the crimson and the gold

By basilisk and bloodstone

By the garlic in the fields

By the poppies and what they yield

Invisibly I make my shield

To detect thee and deflect thee

And to keep thy harm from me

By dragon's blood and salamanders

By horses when their hooves strike sparks

By the dragon breathing flames

From the book of life, I erase thy names

I cut the cords and unlock the chains

I sever all blood ties by which we were bound

With impenetrable walls, myself I surround

Against thy power and its source

Against thy evil and its force

VESTA, PELE, LILITH!

KALI! KALI! KALI!

I banish thee forever from me

And any harm from thee to me

Doubles back and tables turned

Thou shalt by thyself be burned

LILITH! VESTA! PELE!

KALI MA! KALI MA!

By the power of three times three

I banish thee

I banish thee

I banish thee

I am set free, so mote it be!'

The ashes can be buried or washed down a drain. Dispose of all objects that connect you to this person. Be careful with this spell, it is permanent and very powerful.

Cleansing and Purifying Spells

This section deals with spells to cleanse negative energies and purify a person, place or thing.

*Purification Spell for Uncrossing

On the night after a full moon just before bed, light 13 white candles. Fill the tub with hot water, and add one cup of sea salt, one tablespoon of sage, one tablespoon of lavender buds and one tablespoon of chamomile.

Turn off the water and let the herbs steep in the water. Remove your clothes, and kneel before the tub, nude.

Say:

'What was done, was done. Be it now undone.

By the light of the full moon's wane

Cleanse my soul of this stain.

Let not my hurtful spell reverse,

And lift me from the vicious curse.

As i enter now this sacred space

Return mu spirit to its grace.'

Enter the bath and let the water cleanse away the effects of the curse. Use your hands to scoop up the water and pour it three times over the top of your head.

Say:

'Accept my apologies for what was done

Disperse my spell with the morning sun.'

Remain in the bath until the water cools. Drain the tub and rinse yourself off. Snuff out the candles and go to sleep. By dawn the curse will be gone, and you once again feel the blessing that you lost.

Basic Curse Breaking Salt Bath Spell

Fill your tub with warm water. Hold up a container with at least one cup of sea salt and consecrate it by saying:

'In the names of my ancestors, my Gods and myself I call upon thee, Oh creatures of Earth and Water. Come forth and cleanse me of all evil and outside magicks, and restore me to balance and health. By our wills combined, so mote it be!'

Pour the salt into the water, keeping your mind calm and centered. Submerge yourself slowly and soak in the warm salt water, relaxing as much as you can without falling asleep. Let everything slip away.

When the water cools, drain the tub and rinse yourself off with the shower. It is vital that you rinse all the salt down the drain and off your body well. When finished, say:

'I thank you, Oh creatures of Earth and Water, in the name of myself, my Gods and my Ancestors. Be released, doing no harm on your way. Return to me with gladness in

your hearts when next I summon you. By our wills combined, so mote it be!'

Smudging

Smudging is typically associated with Indigenous American Shamanism, although there are many variations of similar rites in many cultures in the form of 'censing'.

Smudging is the practice of cleansing the air, the mind and the emotions with smoke from a sacred plant material- usually sage but sometimes other herbs or resins. With sage, it is scientifically proven that the air is cleansed medicinally. The scent of the smoke has a quite calming effect as well. Any herbs that you choose to use will work best if prepared ahead of time. This is one small way to help raise the energy that you are seeking to utilize for your ritual. If like me, you choose to use fresh grown herbs, when possible, make sure you bundle and hang them upside down in a dry place where they will be undisturbed. This is done by gathering the at the bottom part of the stalk or stem that was cut, and tying them with twine or string, and then hanging upside down, while muttering a prayer, asking them to grant their blessings and magick to your cause. Let them dry for at least a week if possible. It is typically ready to be burned when it cracks and crumbles when you squeeze a piece of it. It must be dried properly to burn properly.

I am going to go with a version that I typically use that isn't exactly of a strict protocol.

*My Variation of a Sage Smudging Ceremony

Make sure that you are personally spiritually prepared before you begin. I usually take a ritual cleansing bath with sea salt and sacred herbs and say a quick self-blessing before starting. This is another way to help raise energy for the ritual. Also, try to make sure you are in a healthy headspace before beginning. You can also listen to some music or drumming to help raise power, or if you have some little ritual that you prefer like meditation that also works amazingly well.

Light the bundle at the thicker end and blow it out when it starts to produce a good amount of smoke.

Rub your hands in the smoke first, to bless and consecrate them to do the good work. Think if it as 'washing your hands' before using them for something important like eating or handling a baby.

I usually use some sort of fan to spread the smoke around easily, this can be a paper hand fan, or even a single large feather. I personally use a small bouquet of feathers that I have found in different places over the years.

Your movement around the room will depend on what you're trying to accomplish. If your goal is to strictly banish negativity or 'evil' influences, I feel it is best to start to the left of your front door and go around the room counterclockwise, following similar suit for each room in the home to the best of your ability. Counterclockwise or widdershins is always best to 'ridding' yourself of something.

If you are doing a general blessing or trying to bring prosperity, luck, health, or anything in the way of good vibes it is best to do the same, except in a clockwise or deosil direction starting at the right of your front door.

When fanning the smoke, it is important to try to let the smoke touch every wall, floor and ceiling in the room or structure. Make sure you have your windows and doors open to let the bad out or the good in.

Concentrate on the doors and windows by tracing the frame of each of them with the smoke well, as if you were washing them or decontaminating. This is basically what the goal is, in a sense. Also, be sure to fumigate the objects in a room, as well as any people. When smudging people, the same rules apply with the widdershins and deosil directions form ridding and drawing. Be sure you start on the left top area (from your perspective) and go counterclockwise for the widdershins rule, and the opposite for the deosil rule.

Also, when cleansing people, be sure you cleanse the mind (around the head), the eyes (Closed if needed as smoke can irritate), the mouth, and the extremities of the body as well as the trunk or torso, front and back.

If there is a specific area on a person or in a place that requires a bit of extra concentration of smoke, you may do this by letting the smoke travel into an upside-down glass vessel that you can see through and sitting it down on top of the area for a moment.

While fumigating with the smoke, be sure you state your intentions. You can do this by telling the negativity to basically *get lost* or by inviting positive vibes or healing and blessing energy in. The same applies for people. Like all other forms of magick, this is all rooted in your intent. Make sure you are thinking clearly and being assertive. You can't really expect it to work if you half-assed do it. You must really apply yourself for it to be truly effective.

When you are finished, remember to ground yourself. Like any other spell or ritual, there will be a lot of excess energy flying around from your work, so unless you want it to keep on flying around, possibly deviating into something you don't want, then you must ground it. This can be done when you get home or away from the place you worked your magick. One way is to just take your shoes and stand on the earth, letting the energy drain into the ground. You can also lay down, meditate or soak in a hot bath or Jacuzzi. The main thing is that you are doing the opposite of what you did to raise that energy- sort of like filling a cup and then emptying it out when you no longer need it.

*Other Types of Herbs and Incense for Smudging and Fumigating

Cedar- calming, comforting, purifying and protection.

Juniper- centering, clarity, cleansing and focus.

Lemongrass- refreshing, communication and channeling.

Pine-cleansing, renewal and strength.

Sage- cleansing, balance, banishing negativity, strengthening and blessing.

Sweetgrass- calling for ancestral spirits, ancient wisdom.

Palo Santo- clears negative energy, aids in physical and psychical healing.

Yerba Santa- protection, setting boundaries.

Rosemary- clears negative energies

Lavender- clears the mind, brings peace, joy and healing to the home. An herb of love and friendship.

Rose Petals- Love and friendship, peace and remembrance.

*Other Powerful Herbs that can be Used in incense and Smudges

Here are a few more herbs that can be used in incense blends, teas and potions, as well as added to your smudge bundles. Some have been previously listed, but here I will list more of their uses, aside from just smudging.

Lavender- Anti-anxiety, clairvoyance, cleansing, love, peace and purifying.

Mint- energy, healing, love, protection, money, psychic powers.

Thyme- affection, clarity, courage, fidelity, healing, psychic powers, purifying.

Sage- cleansing, divination, knowledge, healing, peace, purification and wisdom.

Rosemary- banishing, cleansing, fidelity, happiness, honesty, memory, protection, purifying.

Bay Leaves- wishes, beauty, cleansing, divination, energy, love, luck, purifying.

Basil- confidence, luck, protection, prosperity, warding.

Chamomile- anti-stress, happiness, healing, sleep, love, peace, success.

Vervain- dreams, healing, peace, sleep, love, protection.

Lemon Balm- calming, family, healing, relaxation, success.

*Cleansing By Asperging

Sprinkling liquid on people, places or things to effect spiritual and magickal cleansing. Catholic Priests do this with Holy Water but are certainly not the only ones who employ this method. These Ancient rites direct elemental powers of water or liquid in addition to the properties of herbs (if infused) to a target.

To asperge there aren't really any specific tools that are absolutely required. You can use an Asperger, which is a tool that is made for this purpose, but you can also use something from nature that works just as well, if not better. You can use a small bundle of botanicals, or even a freshly picked stalk of Rosemary. Alternatively, the simplest method is to simply use your fingers to splash the liquid or water onto the target.

The most common Asperging liquids are Holy Water, Florida Water, Four Thieves

Vinegar, Marie Laveau Water, and Rose Water. But you can really use any herbal infusion that you need to. Just remember that some might stain fabrics or other surfaces, so be careful. Some might also burn the eyes or sensitive skin, depending on what is in it, like Four Thieves Vinegar.

Asperging can be done with the same method that I use to smudge, or you can simply splash a little when and where you need it. There really aren't any strict rules aside from using *Intent*.

*New Orleans Voodoo Spirit Cleansing Spell

Place a square of red paper onto a metal or stone dish. You will need one dish for each corner of the room, equaling up to four in most cases.

Place a pinch of sulfur on each red piece of paper.

Place a plate in each corner of the room.

Light the sulfur.

At the same time, address the four Loa invoked in this ritual, turning to face a corner of the room for each one.

Call out:

'Granbois!'

'Baron Carrefour!'

'Baron Cemetiere!'

'Damballah!'

'I invoke you! With the power of your names, I command and compel all evil spirits, spells and vibrations, any negative energies to leave me and my home and never return!'

Withdraw from the room, but be sure to keep an eye on it, as you do not want a fire.

Oye's Cleansing Spell

Oye is the Yoruba Orisha of wild storm winds and the personification of hurricanes. She has the power to blow away all impurities, leaving a fresh and cleansed atmosphere in her wake. She is also the only Orisha in Yoruba who is said to maintain contact and control over the dead. This ritual is used following any unwanted spiritual contact or disturbances.

You will need:

*Nine ribbons of different colors long enough to tie around your waist, plus an additional nine inches of each color.

*Nine small purple eggplants (small enough to fit in the palm of your hand)

*One bottle of red wine

*One bottle of dark rum

*A Cigar

*Nine coins of any denomination

*Wine colored flowers

*White candles

*Sea Salt

Soak the whole eggplants in red wine.

Divide the nine ribbons into three sets of three, braiding each set.

Braid these three sets together into one big, fat braided belt. Tie the additional nine smaller ribbons to the belt so that they will fall around your hips when you wear the belt. Set the belt aside.

Drain and dry the eggplants, and pierce the top of each eggplant, making a hole through it.

Run one of the hanging ribbons on your belt through each one of the eggplants and tie securely, knotting your intentions into the belt.

Take a mouthful of rum and spray it onto the belt.

Light the cigar and blow smoke all over the belt, all the while petitioning Oye to grant your desires.

While this next part is most powerful when done in the nude, do what makes you feel the most comfortable, as I'm sure that the Goddess with Understand.

Tie the belt around your waist. Whirl and twirl around your home, visualizing the negative energy being absorbed into the eggplants.

When you feel like the negative energy is completely gone, take off the belt and place it into a brown paper bag with nine coins.

Take this to Oye's home, the cemetery at night, and leave it at the gates or main entrance. If there are gates, shake and rattle them to make your presence known. If there is no gate, yo may call out to announce yourself. Tell Oye who you are, why you have come and what you need.

Return home a different route than which you came.

Light the white candles in the bathroom and run a bath with warm water and sea salt. Bathe and relax.

When finished, dry off, put on fresh clean clothes and go to bed on fresh clean sheets.

Defensive Magick

This chapter is going to be all about defending yourself or others with magick. There will be several spells to use to deflect evil energy but first there will be methods of detecting, or ascertaining whether it is a curse or the evil eye.

The Evil Eye is basically when someone throws shade at you so hard that it instantly curses you, even if it is unintentional. In fact, many times it is not done on purpose. This can cause bad luck, misfortune, negative energy and sometimes even illness.

*Traditional signs of Evil Eye (or Malocchio, in Italian) attack are:

-Sudden disaster- everything will seem to be going well, then suddenly a major problematic event will trigger a series of other problems to strike.

-Not all attacks are all that sudden. The Evil Eye can manifest as malaise, a lack of energy, a general loss of interest in things, and wasting illnesses.

-Parasites- a pestilence like recurrent headlice or worms that seem to come out of nowhere.

-The Evil Eye can also cause infertility.

-Also: Crops may fail, Animals may die off without explanation, excessive presence of pestilence-like insects, a string of very bad luck.

*Methods of Avoiding the Evil Eye

Don't brag, boast or call undue attention to good fortune.

Protection by using magickal amulets or talismans and spells or chants.

Use discretion when talking about your personal life. (Speak Little, Listen Much- wise words from the Wiccan Rede)

The Italian Jettatura is a person who knows they cast the Evil Eye, because it happens often, uncontrollably. They can't help it, it just emanates from them, but many people don't even realize that they do this. I personally think that this is a malevolent form of psychic vampirism. In fact, I have known and even worked with people afflicted with this malady. It can really be exhausting.

The people most vulnerable to the Evil Eye are usually babies, children, pregnant women, and the elderly. Men are not usually that vulnerable inherently, but their genitals, sperm and capacity for reproduction may be.

*Evil Eye Diagnosis #1

This method will require nine cloves and a glass of cool and clean water.

The curer, or person doing the diagnosis will take nine cloves in the right hand and pass them over and all around the target's head. Light a candle, preferably white for purity.

Insert a pin or a needle through the head and light it over the candle's flame. Use the burning clove to make the sign of the cross over the afflicted person.

Chant:

'Three saw you, three bewitched you

From your mother, you were born

In the name of the father, the son and the holy spirit-

All evil, Go away!'

Drop the burning clove into the glass of water.

Repeat with another clove. If the clove bursts, this is a sign that you have been hit by the Evil Eye. If the person flinches at the sound of the clove exploding or popping sound of the clove bursting, the spell is broken. It is the departing evil that causes the involuntary movement. If no cloves snap, there is no evil detected and any ailments are stemming from other causes. This means you should no longer need to continue the ritual.

If the clove that snaps is the ninth one, three more cloves must be burned. If the third one of these snaps, then burn three more, repeat until there is no more snapping.

The victim must now take three sips from the glass with the burnt cloves in it. They must take a sip from a different spot on the glass.

After this, the curer will face the victim and dip his or her fingers into the glass and sprinkle water in all directions. This must be done a total of three times.

The curer will then dip their fingers into the water again and anoint the victim's forehead with a cross three times, and then do the same on the back of the neck.

*Evil Eye Diagnosis #2 with Olive Oil

Have the victim swish a mouthful of water in their mouth for thirty-three seconds, then spit it onto a small dish or into a small bowl.

Drip three drops of olive oil into the dish of water and watch what happens.

Oil and water don't mix. If the three drops remain distinct, everything is fine. If they disperse, the Evil Eye is present.

*Regarding Protection from the Evil Eye

Many Evil Eye amulets also ward off other dangers like malevolent magick, spiritual attack, etc... Each type of disaster leaves you susceptible to others.

Because the Evil Eye is typically inflicted during close contact, most repelling charms are mobile objects like amulets and conjure bags.

You can never be sure when the Evil Eye attacks, the charms will work independently once they are charged without further action from the spell caster.

Anyone who is particularly vulnerable to the Evil Eye may be protected before they are afflicted by using precautionary measures.

Like healing and cleansing spells, Evil Eye removal spells require the participation of a third party, like a Shaman, Healer, Witch, Priest or Priestess, or a curer on the behalf of the afflicted. Always select ritual assistance carefully. The target of the spell is usually the only affected by it.

Some people believe that tenth commandment in the bible is referring to the Evil Eye when it mentions 'coveting'.

Many Ancients thought that Blue Eyes (which were rare in those regions during those times) were the root of the Evil Eye. This is why you see many amulets that are in the form of big blue eyes. This is a way of deflecting the curse by making it think that you are already afflicted.

*Evil Eye Protection

*Antler Charm-

Attach a piece of antler to a cord made from the braided hairs from a black mare's tail and wear it as a necklace. To make it more powerful, dip the tip of the antler in molten silver. This will balance the energy, as the antler is male energy, and the silver will add female energy. If it breaks, it means that the spell worked, and the curse is broken.

*Eye for an Eye Amulets

Wear a single blue bead on a string around your neck.

Pin several individual blue beads all over your clothing using safety pins.

Sew them onto your clothing or conjure bags.

Hang them from your rearview mirror in your car.

Many people have large glass beads that are disk shaped and look like a large blue eye that they hang up in their home. Not only is it pretty, but functional.

-If a bead cracks or breaks, it means it has worked and can be disposed of. If a soldier in the military has this happen, give it a proper burial.

*Genitalia Amulets

These are said to work because they represent the Life Force. Amulets must be worn visibly to be effective. There are many variations of these amulets that do not look obscene or vulgar. The downward triangle represents the vulva, as do diamond shapes, horseshoes and seashells. A pair of horns can represent internal female sex organs, and a single horn can represent a penis. Also, a stone called Shiva's Lingham that is shaped somewhat like a football with more rounded ends. It is usually banded with shades of brown and tan.

Chili peppers are very potent charms, if pierced and worn as a necklace. It lasts for as long as it stays firm, like the object that it represents. You could use dried chili pepper to avoid impotence.

Cowrie shells look like vaginas, so they are packed with feminine energy. Wear one on a red cord like a necklace. If you are pregnant, make it long enough to wear as a belt to protect your baby. You could also sew blue glass beads and cowrie shells onto a snakeskin and wear it as belt, if you have the stomach for it. (Or not, depending on your interpretation on this)

Winged Phalluses were found in the ruins of Pompeii and were worn and used as home decor for protection.

There are also hand gestures that protect you from the Evil Eye. These are a universal magickal charm that can depict as realistic or have an eye in the palm and be ornate (like the Hamsa)

Fica is what is known as the fig hand. An Italian amulet that depicts a fist balled up with the thumb sticking up between the index and middle fingers. Like the traditional 'I got your nose' gesture. This is said to represent the act of sex, and the word fig is slang for the Vulva.

Mano Cornuto is the horned hand, that basically looks like what my husband does every time we hear a Metallica song. The first and last finger are extended straight up, while the rest of the fist is closed.

Both gestures can be used to ward off the Evil Eye, at any time. A lot of people think I'm a Metal Head, but I kind of just wanna stay safe from Evil Eye Shade Throwers. I am sort of a Metal Head, too.

Bean Spell- growing beans around your property is said to ward off the Evil Eye.

Conjure bags will protect you from the Evil Eye but may not work if you are already afflicted. In India, a red bag containing crocodile teeth, pottery shards, protective verses on paper, chili peppers and lemons or limes are employed as protection.

Another bag that works for this is a red bag with henna, red dirt, iron flakes, and tar. This is worn or kept on the person.

Crossroads Conjure Bag will need dirt from a three-way crossroads that is placed in a red, blue or reflective bag and worn around the neck.

Crescent Moon Charms worn work great as protection. The crescent moon resembles two horns.

Dill sprigs hung over the entrances of your home ward it off as well.

*Evil Eye Detection Egg Spell

This method is used in many Latin and Romany Cultures. Fresh eggs from a local farm work are the best.

Pass one egg around the afflicted person, going over their face, neck, heart, stomach, groin, legs and then back up and around the outline of their body. Do this three times.

With a blessed white candle lit, crack the egg into a bowl and look for dark spots or blood. If any are found, further actions will need to be taken and you must dispose of the egg remains far away from your home.

*Egg and Oil Removal Spell

Fill a metal, stone or glass bowl with Olive oil.

Rub the body from head to toe with five raw eggs, one at a time, using only downward and outward motions.

After each egg has been used, place it in the bowl of oil.

Once all the eggs have been used, Sprinkle them Cayenne Pepper and Cinnamon.

Insert a Cotton Wick and burn off the oil.
When the oil is gone, the spell is complete.

*Egg and Thorn Removal

Gently rub a raw, unbroken egg over the afflicted person's body, especially over the eyes.

Break the egg into a bowl.

Pierce the yoke with seven thorns.

*Evil Eye Salt Removal

Prepare a fire.

Pass a handful of salt around the target's head three times.

Toss the salt into the fire.

*Four Corners Dirt Spell

Take dirt from the four corners of your home on the outside.

Mix it together and toss it on to an open fire shouting:

'Evil Eye, Get the Hell Out and Be Gone Forever!'

*Nine Nail Lemon Spell

Pierce a lemon with nine nails.

Wind red thread around these nails.

Knot the end of the thread around one of the nails.

Place it above the door to repel the Evil Eye.

*Pomander Against Malocchio

Choose an eye shaped citrus fruit- a lemon, lime or citron.

Completely pierce it with holes. Visualize that you're piercing the Evil Eye.

Stuff each hole with a clove. Cloves are like magickal nails.

Bind the pomander with blue or red ribbons and hang it as a warning to the eye of what will happen should it return.

<u>*Old Italian Spell to Remove the Evil Eye</u>

Put three drops of Holy Water or Spring water into a small bowl or saucer.

Add three drops of olive oil to the water, plus seven small leaves from an olive tree that was blessed on Palm Sunday.

Dip your fingers into the mix and swirl the ingredients around, then use a finger to make a cross on the victim's forehead, saying:

'In the Name of Jesus, and Mary and Joseph- Go Away Evil Eye!'

Repeat it twice more.

Repeat this ritual on three consecutive mornings. The oil and water should remain visibly distinct from each other, as they do not naturally blend, so if they do, something is wrong. Should they disperse, immediately throw the water/oil blend away, wait 24 hours and repeat the entire ritual.

Alternative Chant:

'Two eyes have overlooked you,

Two saints have enjoyed you,

By the father, The Son and The Holy Spirit

EVIL EYE BE GONE!'

*Three-Forked Stick Spell (A Gypsy/Romany Spell)

Fill a pot or cauldron with water from a stream. The water must be taken with the current, not against it.

Add the following to the cauldron: seven glowing coals, seven handfuls of cornmeal and seven cloves of garlic.

Place the pot over a fire to boil the brew.

When it comes to boil, stir it with a three-forked stick.

Chant:

'Hey! Evil Eye! Look Here!

Your power is gone.

Seven Ravens come.

Seven Ravens pierce all Evil Eyes, every single one!

Evil Eye! Look Here!

Your Power is now gone!

Dust in your eyes!

You are blind!

Hey! Evil Eye- Look Here!

You are extinguished now!

Burn, Burn, Burn in the fire

Of Kali's vengeance!'

*Send Back the Evil Eye Spell

This ritual will either neutralize the Evil Eye or send it back from whence it came.

If you know who cast the Evil Eye on you, cut out a small piece of their clothing.

Burn it together with frankincense resin.

Brandish the burning incense or the left-over ash remains to the original sender. There is no need to explicitly inform them of your intent. The results are the same and the effect is subliminal.

*Send it Back #2

Sometimes you can feel the Evil Eye right away. It can be neutralized immediately with a very simple ritual from modern day Egypt. Toss a handful of dirt in their wake as they wake away from you. It's as simple as that.

*Who Cast the Evil Eye?

This is a form a divination from Turkey to find out who afflicted you with the Evil Eye.

Light a white candle.

Stick a needle or sewing pin through a clove and pass it through or just above the flame.

As the clove roasts, recite the names of people you suspect of casting the evil eye, repeat in the same order the roasting is going slow and only if necessary.

If the clove should explode as you say a name, this indicates that the culprit has been identified.

*Who Cast the Eye #2

This is the Greek version of this divination. It is quite similar.

Light a white candle.

Stick a needle through a clove and pass over the fire.

Ask Questions regarding the affliction, the cure and the possible caster. (Examples- Male or Female Caster? Should I cast this spell to remove it? Etc...)

Should a clove pop immediately after or during a question, the answer is affirmative.

*Dragon Altar

To remove a persistent case of the Evil Eye, erect a Dragon Altar with an image of a fierce looking dragon with its eyes wide open.

Create a lair to invite the Dragon's presence. Offer treasure to guard; crystals, gold coins (replicas will do) and gemstone beads.

When the Dragon is happy and comfortable, explain your dilemma and that he is the only one strong enough to destroy and consume the Eye.

Visualizations before you go to sleep at night can be especially effective.

Hexes and Offensive Magick

At the risk of sounding like an idiot, I will say this only once. I do not recommend Hexing People. Karma tends to love a good wrestling match with people who think that they are immune to its rules. I am adding these because when I was a young woman in my early 20's I was one of those people, therefore it is in my book of shadows, and I swore to myself that I would include everything that I have in there, even from when I was foolish.

Many of these are kind of out there, and some are quite extreme. Be cautious.

With that being said- I do not feel it's quite as bad if you are enacting a little help to karmic justice, as it does tend to take a while to kick in for many cases. In other words- if you are getting even, YOU'RE not the asshole who started it in the first place, but you can damn sure be the one to finish it. Just don't forget the rule of three. What you send out does come back, so be very careful. There are only so many loopholes that you can use when wording your spells.

You have been warned.

*Candle Spell with Valerian Root

Blend asafetida, cayenne pepper and ground valerian root. Sprinkle over your enemy's photograph.

If you cannot access a photo, write their name in all known variations and as much vital information as you have (age, address, etc...) on a piece of paper.

Place a black candle on top of this and burn it.

*Russian Coffin Hex

Work a strand of your target's hair into wax or some clay. If the clay is from their footprint, it will be even more effective.

Mold or shape the wax or clay into something resembling your target.

Place this image inside a little coffin. A shoebox painted black will work.

Bury this coffin and place a rock over it.

*Coffin Nail Hex

Pound a coffin nail through a piece of fabric soaked in your target's sweat, simultaneously articulate a curse.

*Crossing Oil

Grind a cayenne pepper, grains of paradise, and wormwood together with a mortar and pestle.

Place in a bottle with a pebble from a cemetery.

Cover it with Mineral Oil. Baby Oil works just well.

*Voodoo Doll Hex

This is the basic version of what most people categorize as the stereotypical voodoo doll spell. This is a Gypsy/Romany version that I stumbled upon many moons ago.

Create a figure to represent your target from wax.

Add bits of their clothing, or any intimate items you have (hair from their brush, bristles from their toothbrush, a tiny piece of paper with their handwriting, a small photo, etc...)

When the doll is done, allow it to dry and harden.

Prick it with needles or sewing pins as the spirit moves you, but always prick it a series of three or nine, as these are magickal numbers.

*Doll Hex #2

Create a wax or clay image of your enemy.

Instead of pins and needles, stab it with cactus thorns, while muttering curses against your enemy.

*Doll Hex #3- Footprint Spell

This spell from Malasia combines a wax doll with Foot Track Magick to craft a very potent Hex.

Measure your enemy's footprint. Make a wax effigy of them corresponding exactly in length with the footprint. Add a little dirt from the footprint, personalize it to resemble them in some way and pierce as you wish.

*Malay Paperdoll Hex

This spell is to be done against romantic rivals and suggests making a paper doll to represent your rival, a drawing or a photo will work as well.

Stick a needle in the heart or head, with wishes of misfortune. This will keep her distracted, so she doesn't pursue your man.

*Breakup Spell

This spell is intended to cause animosity between two people who are intimate, either romantically or through business.

Boil a black hen's egg in your own urine. Feed half of it to a dog and the other half to a cat.

Say:

'As these two have a natural hate for each other, so may a natural hate fall between _____ and _____.'

*Dysfunctional Home Hex

To sew general discord within a home, bury a found crow's feather in the target's house. Place it under a potted plant, under a door mat, etc...

It must be a found feather, as taking one by force will cause the spell to backfire. This spell is from India, you may put in under their front steps if you want, so long as they come into a close proximity of it daily.

*Seven Ant Hills Hex

To cause animosity between a couple, collect dirt from seven ant hills and place some between their bedsheets.

*German Footprint Hex

Gather dirt from your enemy's footprint.

Place it in a ceramic pot with a nail, a needle and some shard of glass.

Heat it over a fire until it cracks or breaks.

*Nail Them Down Hex

Hold coffin nails in your hand and focus on your desired result.

Hammer the nails, crosswise above or over the footprint of the one you wish to be tormented.

*Goofer Dust

Some ways to use Goofer Dust-

Toss a handful behind someone's back as they walk away from you.

Sprinkle some in their footprints, or across the path where they will walk.

*Goofer Dust Candle Hex

Slice the top off a black pillar candle so it's flat.

Carve the bottom of the candle so that the wick is accessible and may be lit, effectively reversing the candle.

Carve and dress the candle as you see fit.

Place the candle on a saucer that is sprinkled with goofer dust and burn it, concentrating on your desires.

*Jackballs

This is a Goofer Dust Spell.

Carve and dress a black candle to suit your needs.

Take some of the melted wax and roll it up in the palm of your hand.

Add identifying items of your target to it and continue to roll up.

Add a few drops of your own urine as a controlling mechanism.

Add some goofer dust.

Roll everything into a smooth ball.

Bury it on the target's property.

*Hand Hex

Collect dirt from your enemy's footprint, with nail clippings, hair, etc... whatever you can access.

Place these items into a red flannel conjure bag with a drawstring.

Add graveyard dirt, goofer dust, red pepper, needles, pins, broken glass, rusty nails, as many if these as yo can get.

Bury the bag on their property, at a crossroads, at some old ruins or in a cemetery.

*Hemlock Hex

Write your target's name on a piece of paper using blood from your finger.

Tie the paper around a piece of hemlock and bury it.

*Heart Hex

Obtain an animal's heart- the bigger the better. Purchase a cow heart from a butcher. You can even use a large turkey heart that you put aside when preparing a roast bird one night, or if you know a deer hunter, ask them to give you the heart.

Make nine slits in it.

Write the target's name on nine slips of brown paper.

Place on inside each slit.

Close up with a pair of crossed needles, totaling eighteen.

Wrap the heart up in baker's string or cord.

Blend equal parts of pure grain alcohol with your target's favorite alcoholic beverage. If unsure, just use whiskey.

Place the heart in a jar large enough for it and fill it with the alcohol.

Burn a black candle on top of the jar each night for nine consecutive nights, equaling nine black candles.

When the spell is complete, dispose of the jar far away from your home by burying it somewhere secluded. Return home a different route than that from which you came.

*Hex Ball

Carve and dress a candle.

Burn it against your enemy.

Reserve some melted wax.

Add some mold to it. I have used bread mold, but any kind will work I suppose.

Roll it into a ball and then roll it in some black pepper and ground valerian, effectively coating it well.

Toss the ball onto your enemy's property.

*Hex Conjure Bag

Rip up a photo of your enemy and place it inside a conjure bag.

Add sharp objects like glass shards, nails, pins or needles.

Sprinkle graveyard dirt into it.

If you have burned candles against them, add the wax remnants.

Spit in the bag three times and tightly tie it closed.

Bury it at a crossroads, a cemetery or on their property.

*Hex Packet

Write your enemy's name in black ink on red paper.

Sprinkle asafetida, black salt, camphor, and goofer dust onto the paper.

Fold the paper away from you, knot it shut with red thread and wrap it in black fabric.

Pierce this packet with nine needles.

Bury it on their property where they walk over it.

*Name Paper Hex

Write your enemy's name on a piece of paper clearly with other identifying information.

Dress it with a drop of commanding oil.

Hold it in your hands. Close your eyes and focus on your desires.

Now do something to it to demonstrate an injury to your enemy, for instance stomp on it or stab it.

*Name Paper Lemon Hex

Write the full name of your enemy on a piece of paper. Stick pins through the paper and onto a lemon. This will cause their life to sour.

*Bottle Hex

Place your target's photo into a glass bottle.

Write their name on a piece of paper and add it to the bottle.

Stuff holly and ivy into it.

Add black ink and war water.

Seal it and bury it upside down.

*Black Powder Candle Hex

Grate charcoal until you have fine dust. It must be real coal.

Blend the coal dust with black salt and goofer dust.

Carve a purple candle as desired, then slice the top off and flip over upside-down.

Rub olive oil into your hands and dress the candle with it, starting at the (new) bottom, going to the (new) top of the candle, away from you.

Roll it in the black powder, then set it on a plate and light the candle.

Get completely undressed, remove all jewelry and loosen your hair.

Get in touch with all your inner rage and anger, focus this on your target.

Stick one hundred pins into the burning candle, scream, shout and curse.

When the candle has burned out and the spell is complete, leave all the spell remnants on your target's doorstep.

*Pagan Memorial Candle Hex

Carve and dress a black candle.

Chant what you envision happening to your target.

The idea is to mock a death memorial service, so it wouldn't hurt to set up a mock altar to them, as if they have died- with a picture or personal belongings.

Use a black altar cloth as well.

Let the candle burn down and get rid of the leftovers.

*Skull Candle Hex

This one requires a candle shaped like a human skull.

Carve a skull candle with your target's name and any identifying information you have.

Dress it as desired.

Write the same information on a piece of paper, together with any information that you feel the universe needs to hear about them.

Place the paper underneath the skull candle and light the candles wick.

Stay with the candle as long as it is burning, looking into the eye holes and focusing on what you desire.

When the spell is over, dispose of the remnants outside of your home.

*Public Coffin Hex with Liver

Craft a miniature coffin and paint it black.

Instead of creating a wax doll, place a raw chicken liver inside of it.

Sprinkle asafetida powder and cayenne pepper onto it. Add candle stubs if you want.

Leave it on your enemy's doorstep.

*Egg Hex

Write your enemy's name on a raw egg's shell in blood.

Toss the egg on their doorstep.

*Witch Bottle Hex

Fill a bottle with some of your enemy's hair, nail clippings and/or intimate items belonging to them.

Cut a heart from a piece of red felt.

Stab it with several pins, focusing on the curse.

Stuff the heart inside the bottle and seal it tightly.

Bury it or toss it into a river that is flowing away from you.

*Wormwood Hex

This spell will bring bitterness to your enemy's door.

Powder up some wormwood and sprinkle it across their threshold, focusing your intent on destroying them.

*Hex Breakers and Reversals

Protection Bottle- Place a single castor bean inside of a small glass bottle.

Seal it tightly. Make one bottle with one bean in it for each room in your house.

Replace the bean at every new moon.

<u>Hoodoo Jinx Removal-</u> Place equal parts, one ounce each of cornmeal, salt and your own urine inside a can. A used vegetable can will work.

Put the can on the stove at midnight.

Cook it until its scorched and burned and begins to smell bad.

Dispose of the can and its contents outside of your home.

Domestic Abuse Spells

*Bamboo Protection Spell- Bury a bamboo cane in a cemetery at night. Dig it up the next day, then slip it into your husband's (Or whomever is responsible for your misery) bed while he sleeps. This is a magickal attempt to make him stop beating you.

*Fiery Wall of Protection- Soak a cotton ball in 'Fiery Wall of Protection' Oil.

Tuck it into your pocket or inside your bra.

Pay attention, the smell of it will intensify when danger is eminent.

*Lavender Safety Spells-

-Add Lavender essential oil to your bath.

-safety pin a sprig of lavender to your clothing.

<u>*Spiritual Help-</u>

-Archangel Michael- he offers protection in all areas; however, he is especially known for protection against rape. Call him by name or attract him by burning frankincense and tell him what you need.

-Juno- Burn orrisroot powder on a lit charcoal and offer Juno a rose. Tell her what you need. She specializes in marital abuse.

-St. Rita- Her traditional offering is a bouquet of roses. She protects abused women. Her feast day is May 22.

-Yemaya- She was raped and abused, so it doesn't tolerate it happening to other women. Here is how to gain her assistance:

Petition her at the beach.

Make an altar for her in the sand and burn seven blue candles.

Enter the sea with a bouquet of white roses tied with blue ribbons.

Tell Yemaya what you need and place the roses in the water to be carried off to sea to her.

If you can't go to the sea, put sea salt in water in a goblet on your altar. Light seven blue candles. Bathe in salt water, and soak in it. Tell her what you need. If possible, maintain the white roses on the Altar beside the goblet of 'sea'.

Ancestral Magick

Most Cultures from all over the world usually have one thing in common. That the souls of our Ancestors watch over us and can gently guide us in our times of need, like guardian angels, or may be called upon and/or honored to summon their presence when needed. Not all beliefs are centered around this, but many, many are. To believe in the afterlife, one must accept that spiritual consciousness exists. This would include the belief that there is a way to communicate with the souls of the departed in some way.

According to Chinese Philosophy, some illnesses or other misfortunes may be caused by ancestral spirits. The ancestors may be ill at ease because a grave is neglected, or perhaps misfortunes are happening because there haven't been sufficient offerings made to help maintain their beneficial energy. (Hungry Ghosts) These ancestors aren't necessarily evil, but they may lack the energy to keep evil forces at bay. When they are neglected, they tend to lose power and if forgotten will simply cease to exist on some level. Here are a few ideas that may help your neglected ancestral spirits regain some of that energy.

-You must feed them and feed them well. Ghosts or spirits are basically like a form of wild energy. As we all know, energy cannot be destroyed, but it can change form. Imagine being extremely 'Hangry' and being psychokinetic. You get the picture.

-Check to see if their grave site is in order or needs tending. Make any improvements you can. If this isn't possible for you, like if it is too far away or doesn't exist, explain this to your ancestors in detail, and tell them what you plan to do to rectify this situation. You may need to use a form of divination to receive any kind of feedback from them on this matter.

-Build an Ancestral Altar. If you already have one erected, make some updates to it and try to make it as aesthetically pleasing to them as possible.

-Burn Paper Offerings. Traditionally, Spirit Money (Hell Money or Banknotes of Hell) are burned, effectively sending them over to the other side for our ancestors to use to make their afterlife a little more comfortable. They also like mail. You can write them a letter or even print out some photos to send them if the mood strikes you. The smoke from the items burning will carry them to the afterlife.

To Set Up an Ancestral Altar

Find a good spot to set up your altar. A small table or shelf usually suffice for this.

Arrange photos, place personal items that belonged to them or something that would remind them of their connection to us. If they have a favorite flower, you could put a small vase there, a favorite ring that they wore, a lock of their hair if you have it, or if they loved cats, you could put a little cat figurine up there. The possibilities are endless. It just depends on your resources, space and what you think their preferences would be.

Place a white candle on the altar, I would suggest a glass jar candle for safety reasons. Next to it place a glass of clean spring water and make any other offerings that you deem fit. Fruit is a great choice, and sometimes I put out a small dish of treats. My dad liked to have a drink of whiskey every now and then, so I sometimes pour a shot for him and lay an unlit cigarette beside it. He did love his vices.

Light the candle and some incense. Burn some Hell Money in generous amounts. This usually appeases the Ancestors more than you would think it would. It's the little things that count, even in the afterlife.

Ghosts and Spirits

If you are reading this book, it's probably a safe bet to assume that you believe in spirits or ghosts. The power of belief is a very potent thing. I feel that we manifest so much just by faith or willpower alone, and this includes the things we don't necessarily want. An example of this is when someone is using a Ouija board with a group of friends at a party to try to contact their deceased auntie. Usually there is one in the group that absolutely refuses to acknowledge anything that isn't 100% tangible. This person usually will not be very willing to accept any signs from any Spiritual entities, and therefore will push the idea immediately aside by trying to rationalize anything that happens that wasn't caused by deliberate human actions.

My thoughts on this are as follows: You will not be able to see, if you do not open your eyes. If you keep the blinders of your rationality and one-sided thinking on, then you will be missing out on some amazing phenomena. (Not to get off track here) The gifts of clairvoyance, mediumship or even psychic sensitivity- they are exactly that. GIFTS. A gift is still a gift, even if we do not appreciate it. Moving on.

People are inherently afraid of that which they do not understand or comprehend. I know... A lot of people will not agree when I say this; but the whole thing about books and not judging them by their covers also works for the realm of the dead.

A pop-culture example of this lies in the film, The Sixth Sense.

(SPOILER ALERT) In the film, the boy is terrified of the spirit of a girl in a nightgown that vomits on herself and is clearly not at peace. Initially, he thinks that she wants to harm him, but after talking to his shrink, Bruce Willis he decides to try to find out what is bothering her. When he braces himself and finally stands up to his fears, he finds out that the girl's ghost is simply trying to get a message to her father. They boy goes to the family home for the Wake and the ghost leads him to find a nanny cam that has footage of her own mother poisoning her. Once the boy gives the tape to the father and he pops it into the VCR, he sees what his horrible wife had done. This effectively puts a conclusion to her unfinished business, as now her little sister will be spared the same fate that she suffered. Her spirit, now at ease, no longer seems as terrifying as she did initially to the boy, and she is able to move on. The boy, by facing his fears, was able to resolve her unfinished business and overcome his own fears by taking some initiative and being brave.

This example is not always the case, however. I always tell people, do not trifle with spirits if you are not prepared for what comes next. There is always a risk that they are not what they appear to be. There are other types of energies out there that might present themselves as ghosts but actually be something much more ancient and darker. These dark energies can latch onto you at any time and sometimes for seemingly no reason.

Dark energies aren't always in the form of a specific entity, as sometimes what would seem like a spiritual or demonic attachment may be residual energy that is associated with the past that has somehow become fused to an object or place. An example would be something like Poltergeist activity. Many forms of poltergeist activity are rooted in mental anguish or hormones, but some are literally leftover bad vibes that never properly grounded or dissipated and can be attached to an item, like a curse.

Spiritual attachments of dark entities, or vengeful spirits is also a possibility. Some people are just bad seeds in life, and it carries over to the afterlife. This sort of darkness is a stain that cannot easily be removed. Vengeful spirits are usually very powerful because they are driven by rage or a powerful emotion like sadness or regret that deviates and grows and spreads into something that contaminates everything it comes into contact with. These entities almost always have some sort of unfinished business, but a lot of times it is nearly impossible to resolve it without having to banish the entity, as it has ventured past the point of no return.

Lastly, I will mention Demonic attachment. This is usually not generally accepted by a lot of pagans, as they do not believe that demons exist but I, being the strange and unique religious hybrid that I fully believe that they are indeed, very real and very dangerous. Demons, in the Christian aspect are *basically* hordes of evil entities that the Devil rules over in hell and sometimes they like to dabble in making life as miserable as possible for humans in the land of the living, just to be dicks. This is how many people feel. But having researched demonology over the past 25 years and knowing what I know by what my mother passed down to me (My grandmother was a Demonologist and a Spiritualist) and by reading tons of works about Sir John Dee of medieval England and tons of research on King

Soloman's work, I have learned that demons have a hierarchical society. Each demon, like the saints, has a specific 'specialty'. For instance; 'Valak' from the movies (The Nun and Annabelle, etc...) featuring Ed and Loraine Warren's extensive work (although very much padded with fictitious elements) is based on Valac, who is described in the Lesser Key of Solomon. Valac is said to be a 'prince of hell' or a high-ranking demon who can control or command snakes as well as household spirits. He allegedly leads around 30 legions of demons.

There are differing accounts in numerous tomes that discuss these demons, including Johann Weyer's *Pseudomonarchia Daemonum,* written in 1583. He estimated that in this complicated calculation of the hierarchies that the number of demons is 4,439,622 and they are divided into 666 legions, with each legion consisting of 6,666 demons with all of them being ruled by 66 Dukes, Princes, Kings and Generals.

Several branches of Occultism say that there are seven devils that represent the seven deadly sins:

Lucifer- who represents pride.

Mammon- greed.

Asmodeus- lust.

Leviathan- envy.

Beelzebub- gluttony.

Satan- wrath.

Belphegor- sloth.

These are supposedly the most powerful of the demons.

There are signs and warnings to watch out for that will foretell a spirit or demon attaching itself to you.

Many of the signs between the two are similar, but I am going to focus on the spiritual aspect of attachments. We will save the subject of demonology for another book.

*A Few Signs that a Ghost is Present

Candles that burn dim, low or blue flames with no explanation.

Cold spots or a sudden chill in the air.

Ghosts may also indicate their presence with a smell or fragrance, usually something associated with their life on the earthly plane. (a favorite perfume or maybe even cigar smoke)

Seeing them- sometimes ghosts show themselves to us, but it takes a lot of energy for them to do this intentionally, and usually they will barely be visible.

Audible communications from them- Personally, I have heard whispers, usually at night when I go to lay in my bed and sometimes just out of the blue throughout the day. Sometimes it is unintelligible, and a lot of times I can clearly hear simple 1–2-word phrases, like 'wake up' or even my name.

Witnessing doors, windows, cabinets, etc... open or close by some unseen force.

Electrical disturbances that cannot otherwise be scientifically explained.

The general feeling that someone is watching you or hoovering in your personal space when there is nobody physically present.

*Hungry Ghosts

Many ancient cultures believe that ghosts become mischievous when they have nobody to feel or honor their memory. In China, August is Hungry Ghost Month- a time when unsettled ghosts are more likely make their grievances known to us.

It is usually a good idea to leave them offering to tame their mischief.

Some people bury apples at a crossroads on Halloween (Samhain) to feed hungry ghosts. Mesopotamians would leave regular offerings of flour and fresh water to keep them satisfied. The Celts left honey and barley for them.

*Rest in Peace Spell

Restless ghosts may be laid to rest by having a funeral service for them. Fashion a small doll in their likeness and baptize it in their name or alternatively dedicate it to them. Place it into a small coffin or a decorated shoebox and bury it in sacred ground if possible. If you can't, then simply bless a small area of your yard to this purpose and use it for this purpose. Say a few words of peace and send them on their way.

*Putting the Dead to work- a General Spell

This practice's roots date back to ancient Egypt but have a hoodoo twist.

Set up an altar dedicated to the spirit you are requesting help from. This can be anywhere in your home.

The minimal offering is a white candle and a glass of fresh spring water.

The altar may also be personalized more to form a stronger psychic bond with the spirit. Like an Ancestral Altar.

Write a brief clear and concise statement of your desires on a brown piece of paper. Place this in a conjure bag with graveyard dirt and seven coffin nails.

Coffin nails are basically tapered upholstery nails that have been prepared by being buried in graveyard dirt. I do not advise digging up a grave and busting up any coffins in order to get this supply.

Carry this with you as an amulet, when your wish is granted, bury it in the earth.

*Afrit Banishing Spell

Afrit, a malevolent Egyptian/Middle eastern spirit rises from the ground when the blood of a murder victim is shed. An afrit may be restrained by driving a virgin nail (never used) into the ground in the exact spot where the murder was committed. To release the afrit, remove the nail.

*Bamboo Banishing Spell

This spell from Korea banishes unwanted house spirits.

Burn bamboo sticks. The sound of the popping knots scares house demons away.

*Bean Banishing

Fill rattles with dry beans and shake then to drive away low-level entities. This may be incorporated into rituals as needed for added protection.

*Botanical Spirit Banishing

Plants that make malevolent Spirits feel unwelcome:

Juniper

Maize/ Corn

Mugwort

Saint John's Wort

Vervain

Wormwood

Yarrow

-Incense to Disperse Evil- burn benzoin, patchouli and sandalwood to disperse malicious spirits.

Exorcism Spells

#1 Exorcism Spell

Use intensive cleansing methods to purify the area.

Ring bells, cymbals or tambourines loudly.

Invoke benevolent, protective spirits. Kwan Yin, St. Michael the Archangel or Isis are some good ones.

Draw up a protection talisman, this can be as simple as a cross or a pentacle, but the more work and intent you put into it, the better.

Summon the demons, demanding that they show themselves and depart. This may take a little work on your part, as they usually don't want to leave.

Observe for sign of departure, dramatic spirits will make this very clear, but sometimes the signs are subtle.

If you are certain that they have departed, then you may burn the talismans.

Mix a tablespoon of the ashes into cooled boiled spring water. Have the afflicted person drink it.

Close the ceremony.

Exorcism Spell #2

Fill a new pot with freshly drawn water.

Pour some olive oil onto the water.

Whisper Psalm 10 over the water nine times.

Dip a new towel into the liquid and wash the afflicted person with it.

Exorcism Spell #3

Apply essential oil of frankincense to the crown of the head, the forehead, back of the neck, the throat, chest, palms of the hands and the souls of the feet.

Now add oil to some freshly drawn water.

Using a brand-new towel, bathe all the body parts listed above, as well as the genital area.

Repeat Psalm 145 throughout the ritual.

*Extreme Yang Spell

This spell is not what you're thinking! Get your mind out of the gutter!

In China, traditional belief states that demons come from excessive yin energy. This can be opposed by using potent yang energy. These serve as a demon/ yin repellent.

Firecrackers, mirrors, swords and the crowing of a rooster.

Reading sacred texts and philosophy books is believed to send away malevolent spirits because they create order, which demons cannot thrive in.

*Ginger Banishing Spell

Traditionally it's believed that low-level demons or malevolent spirits can enter the body through food. Certain foods can guard against this. Ginger is thought to expel and prevent these types of demons.

*Low Level Demon Banishment #1

Low level demons are easily fooled. A common practice in the middle east is paint the ceiling a sky blue. This fools the low intellect entity and confuses them, making them depart the property to think about it.

*Low Level Demon Banishment #2

Mirrors- it is generally believed that mirrors are portals to the spirit realm. This is a two-way street. If a demon sees it's reflection in a mirror, it is said to get suck into the mirror rendering it unable to further torment the victim. Ladies, keep your compact handy.

*Incantation Bowl Spell (Mesopotamia)

An incantation bowl is a shallow terracotta dish that is covered entirely with incantations starting at the rim and spiraling inward to the center. An image may be drawn in the center, sometimes a rough sketch of a succubus or a female demon.

The goal is to trap the entity under the dish, where the written incantations will subdue it and render it powerless. The dish is then buried under the doorstep of the home.

These can be purchased or made by hand. Making it yourself tends to make it more powerful, as you are putting more of your energy into it and imbibing it with your intentions.

*Magick Mirror Demon Banishment

This spell is derived from ancient Chinese traditions, the mirror should be a small, handheld round one.

On a bright and sunny day, slowly traverse the afflicted area holding a small mirror in your hand so that every part of the room is reflected to you for a few moments.

Once you have finished, place the mirror face down or wrap it in dark cloth.

Immediately take it outside into the bright light, and suddenly expose it to the sunlight for no more than nine seconds.

Captured negative energies are burned out and destroyed by the light.

The mirror, the area and you now will require a very thorough spiritual cleansing.

*Baron Carrefour's Banishing Spell

Most Crossroads Spirits like Papa Legba, Hermes and Hecate have a very fine line that separates them from being a trickster from being a malevolent spirit. This is especially so for Voodoo Loa, Baron Carrefour- the master of the crossroads. He rules the nocturnal crossroads and is very volatile so he can very easily become dangerous. He isn't typically summoned without a very good reason. If malicious spirits are tormenting you, ask that he deny them access to you. This can be done by offering him a fine quality cigar and a good rum. Be humble and very polite when addressing him. If you annoy him this good all turn bad very easily.

*Mandrake Banishing

Place a mandrake root (or some of the chopped herb, as it is more affordable and accessible) in a room to drive evil spirits out.

*Poltergeist Banishing by Door Slamming

Slamming every door in your home three times will temporarily frighten away poltergeist activity.

*Sage Burning Spirit Spell

Burn White Sage, either by smudging with a sage bundle or placing the dried leaves of the white sage plant onto a charcoal disk. Alternatively, you can just use white sage incense sticks if you need to. This will drive away negative entities.

*Sinistrari's Demon Banishing Advice

Luvidico Sinistrari was a Franciscan Friar and demonologist in the seventeenth century. He said that five ingredients would repel and expel demons. They were Jasper, Jet, castor oil, coral and menstrual blood. Incorporate them into your banishing rituals.

*Trapped in a Bottle Spell

Evil Spirits, such as Djinn may be trapped into a bottle.

Drop 13 thorns into a glass bottle or jar, one at a time.

As you drop each one in, tell the evil to go away, assertively.

Drop rose petals from one rose in, one at a time to cover the thorns.

Fill the jar 2/3 of the way full with holy water or salt water.

Leave the jar open and unattended overnight.

Before sunrise, close the jar and seal it up tightly, the evil should be inside of it.

Wrap it in dark cloth and bury it far away.

*Turmeric Banishing

Sprinkle ground turmeric over burning coal. Malicious spirits can't stand the smell.

*Witch Balls

Globes of iridescent, colored glass. Place them around your home to repel unwanted spirits.

*Woodlands Banishing Spell

Burn acorns, mistletoe and oak bark to repel an undesirable spirit guest, while muttering your desire for them to effectively GTFO.

Please remember to always be responsible when using magick, and remember that there is always a price!

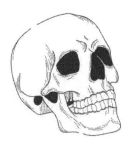

Thank you for reading my book! This book is not verbatim to my grimoire, but it almost is, and I really hope you enjoyed it. I hope it will be a useful addition to your Witchy Library and may it inspire you on your path to enlightenment and finding your way in your own Magickal workings. Or you could just embrace the chaos of my blend of eclectic paganism. Stay tuned for more Mama Nightshade works, I have a lot planned!

Blessed Be!

)0(

~Mama Nightshade

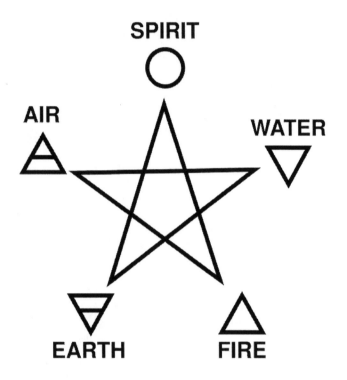

Made in the USA
Columbia, SC
01 December 2024

47372644R00100